Roses

TIME
LIFE
BOOKS
®

Other Publications:

THE SEAFARERS

THE ENCYCLOPEDIA OF COLLECTIBLES

WORLD WAR II

THE GREAT CITIES

HOME REPAIR AND IMPROVEMENT

THE WORLD'S WILD PLACES

THE TIME-LIFE LIBRARY OF BOATING

HUMAN BEHAVIOR

THE ART OF SEWING

THE OLD WEST

THE EMERGENCE OF MAN

THE AMERICAN WILDERNESS

LIFE LIBRARY OF PHOTOGRAPHY

THIS FABULOUS CENTURY

FOODS OF THE WORLD

TIME-LIFE LIBRARY OF AMERICA

TIME-LIFE LIBRARY OF ART

GREAT AGES OF MAN

LIFE SCIENCE LIBRARY

THE LIFE HISTORY OF THE UNITED STATES

TIME READING PROGRAM

LIFE NATURE LIBRARY

LIFE WORLD LIBRARY

FAMILY LIBRARY:
   HOW THINGS WORK IN YOUR HOME
   THE TIME-LIFE BOOK OF THE FAMILY CAR
   THE TIME-LIFE FAMILY LEGAL GUIDE
   THE TIME-LIFE BOOK OF FAMILY FINANCE

Roses

by
JAMES UNDERWOOD CROCKETT
and
the Editors of TIME-LIFE BOOKS

Watercolor Illustrations by
Allianora Rosse

TIME-LIFE BOOKS, ALEXANDRIA, VIRGINIA

THE AUTHOR: James Underwood Crockett, a graduate of the University of Massa-chusetts, received an Honorary Doctor of Science degree from that University and has been cited by the American Association of Nurserymen and the American Horticultural Society. He has worked with plants in California, New York, Texas and New England. He is the author of books on greenhouse, indoor and window-sill gardening, and has written a monthly column for *Horticulture* magazine and a monthly bulletin, *Flowery Talks,* for retail florists. His weekly television program, *Crockett's Victory Garden,* has been seen on public broadcasting stations through-out the United States.

THE ILLUSTRATOR: Allianora Rosse, who provided the delicate, precise watercolors of rose varieties beginning on page 106, is a specialist in flower painting. Trained at the Art Academy of The Hague in The Netherlands, Miss Rosse worked for 16 years as staff artist for *Flower Grower* magazine. Her paintings and drawings of shrubs, trees and flowers have appeared in many books on gardening.

GENERAL CONSULTANTS: Peter Malins, Rosarian, Brooklyn Botanic Garden, New York City; Herbert C. Swim, Ontario, California; Joseph J. Kern, Mentor, Ohio.

THE COVER: A modern hybrid rose, the Lady Bird Johnson, is the spectacular result of an amateur rose breeder's success. The variety was introduced in 1970 after six years of experimentation by Eldon Curtis, a Dallas insurance man and rose hobbyist *(page 93).*

CONTENTS

1 The queen of flowers 7
Picture essay: ROYAL FAMILIES 22

2 Planting, pruning and protection 43
Picture essay: THE ROMANCE OF THE ROSE 72

3 Creating better blooms 85
Picture essay: A BOUQUET OF ARRANGEMENTS 98

4 An illustrated encyclopedia of roses 107

APPENDIX

Characteristics of 344 roses 146

How climate affects rose growing 153

Bibliography 154

Credits and acknowledgments 154

Where to see roses—97 notable gardens open to the public 155

Index 156

The queen of flowers 1

Sooner or later, everyone who has a garden thinks about growing roses. There are practical reasons—if a gardener needs them—for deciding to do just that. For one thing, roses outperform practically every other kind of garden plant in the number of flowers they produce, in the length of their blooming season and in their normal life expectancy. But most gardeners become rose growers simply because they fall in love with the flowers. Roses have an irresistible combination of elegance and charm, thorny strength and satin-petaled delicacy, and their blooms come forth in a wonderful variety of colors, sizes, shapes and fragrances. It is this, the sensuous appeal of roses, that has made them the world's best-known and most popular ornamental plant.

Some people become so attached to roses that they talk to them, as if they were pets. Every once in a while I catch myself muttering words of encouragement to a plant that is slow to leaf out or begin blooming. I don't really believe that this helps the plant in any way, of course, but I must admit that it makes me feel better.

Any book about roses should open with words of encouragement to the beginner, who has perhaps been overwhelmed by the thought that roses make such unique demands on a gardener that growing them may be beyond his ability. Roses do require a certain amount of pampering. Yet it should be reassuring to remember that roses were growing long before there were human hands to tend to their needs. Fossil roses, found in rock formations in Colorado and Oregon, proved that wild roses date back 40 million years. They apparently originated in central Asia and spread all over the northern hemisphere, but inexplicably never crossed the equator—no truly wild roses have been discovered in the southern hemisphere. Almost everywhere else, however, wild roses can be found growing, often under difficult conditions—in the arctic cold of Alaska and Siberia, in the heat of India and North Africa. Wild roses grow in every state, and without much doubt there are some close to your home wherever you live. They thrive in the sand dunes

The hybrid tea rose seen at left in bud and bloom epitomizes this most popular rose, whose blossoms come in a panoply of colors. Many hybrid tea roses have a rich fragrance and often measure 4 inches or more across.

of New England, in the wooded hills of New York, Indiana and Pennsylvania, in the open prairies of Missouri and Iowa and along streams in California.

Many time-honored garden roses are genetically similar to wild roses, but differ from them in that their flowers are larger, more fully petaled or more deeply colored. They are actually mutations of wild plants selected by gardeners over thousands of years. Unlike most garden roses, which are mixed hybrids, these unusual forms of wild roses are of genetically pure strains, although their unique characteristics are not always transferable to seedlings.

The strangest thing about most truly wild roses is that their flowers do not look like roses at all. Instead of the familiar garden plant's bright globes, made up of large numbers of tightly interleaved petals, most wild rosebushes bear flowers that look like apple blossoms—one layer of five petals, a "single" in the horticulturist's term. This open form may help wild roses continue to survive without human care, since it exposes pollen for easy transmission by insects, increasing the chances that the plant will reproduce despite the highly competitive conditions in its natural environment.

Historical records indicate that wild roses were brought under cultivation in China about 5,000 years ago. By the time of the Han dynasties just before the Christian Era, rose gardens had become so popular that huge parks were devoted to them. It is said that land needed for agriculture was tied up, threatening food production and forcing the Emperor to order the destruction of some of the rose parks and to curtail rose culture in others. During this same period the Egyptians did a thriving business growing roses for the Romans, and according to some authorities shipped cut flowers to Rome via galley (how the flowers could be kept fresh for the long trip across the Mediterranean remains a mystery). The Romans were so enamored of roses that they also supported large nurseries in the south of Italy, particularly at Paestum (near the present-day city of Salerno); one order from the Emperor Nero for cut flowers for a night's feast reportedly ran up a bill totaling, in terms of modern currency, about $100,000.

After classical days, the "Queen of Flowers," as the Greeks described the rose, became less valued for its beauty than for its supposed medicinal value. Extracts were made from the dried petals and used in medicines and ointments for all sorts of ailments, though the only good they probably did was to disguise the taste of unpalatable concoctions. Roses for such purposes were produced by monasteries and private growers all over Europe, but the most famous center of culture was at Provins, outside Paris, which maintained its pre-eminence for six centuries—at one point the town's main street was lined with apothecary shops.

All these ancient roses and their descendants are in botanical terms members of a single group, or genus, *Rosa*, that is part of a much larger family of shrubs, herbs and trees known as *Rosaceae*. The rose's close relatives include not only strawberries, raspberries and hawthorn, but such fruits as the peach, almond, apple and apricot. In spite of the superficial differences among them, there are traits that connect them, such as blossoms that generally have petals in sets of five. Many bear edible fruit, and the rose is no exception. After a blossom's petals drop off they leave behind a small, round, usually red "hip." It is the raw material for rose-hip jelly—an old-fashioned favorite in England and New England —and is also an excellent source of vitamin C. (Rose hips were made into syrup to supply vitamin C to children in Britain during World War II, when supplies of citrus fruit, the usual vitamin C foodstuff, were cut off.) The resemblances among the members of the *Rosaceae* family have led some botanists to believe that all were descended from some prehistoric common ancestor, though its identity remains an unsolved mystery.

The ancestors of modern garden roses are easier to trace. The large number of varieties now in existence are, at least in part, descended from eight species of roses that began arriving in Europe from Asia around 1700. These roses entered into modern hybrids

GENEALOGY OF A QUEEN

The complex ancestry of the first and the most famous grandiflora rose, the Queen Elizabeth (pictured on page 119), reveals the multiple crossings that go into the creation of a modern hybrid rose. This chart names only the Queen's more recent ancestors, with their dates of introduction, types and colors. In an attempt to produce a new and more vigorous red rose, Dr. Walter E. Lammerts, a professional plant breeder in California, crossed one of his previous prize winners, the Charlotte Armstrong, with the Floradora, from quite a different lineage. After several tries that produced reddish roses with one defect or another, Dr. Lammerts grew a perfect one—in a glorious pink.

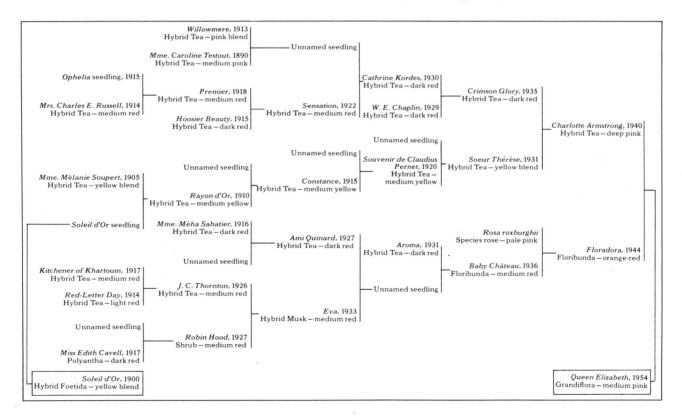

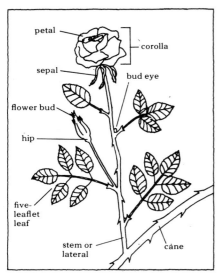

From its winter hiatus the rose in spring changes swiftly into a leafy, blooming plant. The bare canes first send out stems called laterals. Along these sprout the rose's distinctive teardrop-shaped leaflets in clusters—each cluster, which may have one, three, five, seven or nine leaflets, is botanically a single leaf. The stem completes its growth when it forms at its tip a tightly shut bud, or calyx, wrapped in leaflike sepals that curl away as the bud opens into a full blossom called a corolla. Normally, the blossom at the tip of the stem is the first to open. Other blossoms emerge lower down from tiny green "bud eyes," which appear at the bases of those leaves having three or more leaflets.

principally because they possess a feature not commonly found in other roses: an ability to blossom repeatedly throughout the growing season—in some cases all season long—whereas most of the other species blossom just once in June or July. With this valuable attribute, however, some of the Asiatic roses, particularly the tea rose, *R. odorata,* and the China or Bengal rose, *R. chinensis,* carried a less desirable trait: a lack of hardiness. Not only are these two species native to a warm climate and thus inherently tender, but they have a tendency to continue to grow throughout the year. They persist in growing even in the face of frosts, unlike northern plants, which become dormant. They fight dormancy and die, whereas shrubs native to the north simply rest during the cold period of the year. Modern crossbreeding has produced hardy, cold-resistant hybrids from these delicate plants, and today their best qualities can be enjoyed in many areas *(Chapter 4 and map, page 153).*

Some of the best hybrids, however, turned out to have gained their hardiness at the cost of something else. Although they resisted cold, they were weak plants with spindly root systems, lacking in what horticulturists call vigor. The solution to this problem was discovered by pioneering rose growers, who joined the flower-bearing branches of weak but beautiful plants to the vigorous roots of wild roses, creating two plants in one. This practice is carried on today, no longer using roots collected from forests and hedgerows but exceptionally vigorous cultivated rootstocks such as selected forms of the *Rosa multiflora,* or Japanese rose; this grafting technique accounts for the knucklelike lump at the base of most rose plants—the so-called bud union where the root plant and the flowering plant have been joined together.

Toward the end of the 19th Century all except one of the elements of the modern rose had been supplied, but that missing characteristic was a trait longed for by rose growers—an attractive yellow color. There were yellow roses, but none were quite satisfactory. The ones among the recent Asiatic importations were a sulfurous rather than a pure yellow, and others among the wild or semiwild plants were inferior in size or shape.

The clue to the desired yellow turned up in the Parc de la Tête d'Or, the municipal gardens of Lyons, France. Strolling among its rosebushes one summer day in 1885, rose breeder Joseph Pernet-Ducher was struck by the golden shades of a Persian Yellow. Its flowers did not have the desired tea-rose shape, but its genetic traits, Pernet-Ducher decided, could introduce bright yellow into flowers of the hybrid-tea class.

His research took 25 years. After 13 years of crossbreeding he managed to create a still-popular rose, Soleil d'Or, that is light yellow on the outside but orange-red or pink inside. Twelve more years of crossing and back-crossing were necessary before he achieved the first pure yellow garden rose the world had ever seen: Rayon d'Or. From these and related varieties have come all the modern yellow, orange and flame-colored roses.

The value of a discovery such as a new color is so great—royalties may bring the grower millions of dollars—that rose breeding is always surrounded by an aura of romance and adventure. In 1939, when Francis Meilland found a sturdy plant with magnificent pale gold blossoms growing from one seed he had nurtured, he knew he had bred something valuable, but he had no idea how valuable—nor did he realize how long it would take him to find out. He sent cuttings to Germany, Italy and the United States—the bundle of stems addressed to a Pennsylvania rose grower was aboard the last American plane that got out of France in November 1940, a step ahead of the invading Nazis.

Not until World War II ended five years later did Meilland learn that his exported cuttings had been used to propagate the rose that many experts consider the best ever developed, the variety known in the U.S. as Peace. Within a decade the Peace rose was blossoming on more than 30 million bushes throughout the world. "How strange to think," Meilland said, "that all these millions of rosebushes sprang from a tiny seed no bigger than the head of a pin—a seed we might so easily have overlooked or neglected in a moment of inattention, or which might have been relished as a tidbit by some hungry field mouse."

Happily, the crossing, recrossing and back-crossing of roses of the past has produced so many varieties—about 5,000 are now available—that the gardener can find numbers suited to every part of the country and to every use imaginable. There are roses for formal and informal plantings, for landscaping effects and for ensuring privacy, for keeping the garden bright with color and for keeping the home liberally stocked with cut flowers. It is the gardener's pleasant task to choose the roses that are best adapted to his needs and tastes.

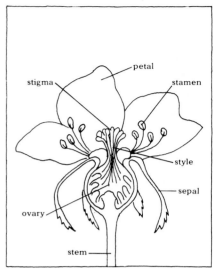

Cupped in the colorful petals of a rose are the reproductive organs that enable the plant to propagate itself from seed. Just inside the petals and their surrounding layer of leaflike sepals are stamens, the male organs, supporting round anthers. After the flower blooms, the anthers split to release pollen grains; these grains cling to the bodies and legs of insects and are carried to a female organ, or pistil—in the same flower or in one that may be far away. The pistil is topped by a trumpet-shaped fuzzy cluster, the stigma; it catches pollen grains, which grow pollen tubes down through the slender column of the style to the ovary. There they fertilize the eggs and produce seeds.

THE FAMILIES OF ROSES

Despite the large number of rose varieties that are now being grown, all can be divided into groups, some classified by type, others by use. The descriptive listing of roses in Chapter 4, which provides information on more than 300 varieties, separates them into nine groups. (The proper botanical term for a hybrid rose created by a rose breeder is "cultivar," but the word "variety" is commonly used, as it is throughout this book.)

By far the most popular today is the hybrid tea, a clearly established type, or class, that offers an exceptional range of color, fragrance, flower size and shape for bouquets and for bright display in the garden. It turned up by chance in the gardens of a professional rose breeder, J. B. Guillot, near Lyons, France, in 1867. Guillot had planted seeds collected from a number of roses, and one of the seedlings surprised him with the beauty of its flower: a sweet, silvery pink rose he named La France. It is believed to be a descendant of the fragrant, bright pink, hybrid perpetual, Madame Victor Verdier, and the fragrant, creamy white tea rose, Madame Bravy—but neither Guillot nor anyone else could tell for certain. At the time of its introduction it was considered to be simply a particularly good hybrid perpetual, and not until 1880 did rose growers decide that it and similar new creations deserved a new class of their own, the hybrid tea.

Floribunda roses are products of the 20th Century, resulting from the mating of polyantha and hybrid tea roses, pioneered by D. T. Poulsen of Denmark, who worked to create a type that would thrive in northern Europe's severe climate. In 1924 Poulsen's son Sven introduced the first outstanding floribunda, the pink Else Poulsen. The floribunda lives up to the meaning of its Latin name, "flowers in abundance," for with ordinary care it will blossom without ceasing from early summer until frost. Floribunda colors cover the gamut of hues from snowy white to sparkling yellow to deep tones of crimson. No other rose is more adaptable to use in numerous garden settings, and no others, with the exception of shrub roses, thrive so well in combination with other kinds of plants.

Grandiflora roses, the product of crosses between hybrid teas and the free-flowering, sturdy floribunda roses, are generally a little taller and hardier than the hybrid teas, with a larger number of slightly smaller flowers. They were developed only recently, but such superb varieties as Queen Elizabeth have rapidly made them very popular.

Climbing roses are not a type of rose by themselves but a category of botanically diverse plants that have long arching or upright canes; many climbers, such as the hybrid tea climbers and the so-called large-flowered climbers, bear big blossoms, while others such as the ramblers and polyantha climbers, have small flowers. The climbers are misnamed in another sense, for no rose possesses tendrils that enable branches to attach themselves to a support; all must be tied to a trellis or wall or draped over it. But they have many uses, practical as well as esthetic. Left to grow as they please, they will clothe a naked embankment or soften the contours of a rocky outcropping. Trained to supports of various kinds, they will conceal an ugly foundation, follow a fence or wall, frame a doorway, climb high trellises and form thick screens in front of exposed patios and swimming pools. One special kind of climber, called a pillar rose, creates a spectacular effect; it has stiff canes that stand up nearly straight 8 feet or more and is usually grown tied to a post.

The rose known as polyantha, or occasionally as baby rambler, was created during the last quarter of the 19th Century by crossing dwarf forms of the China rose, *R. chinensis,* and the Japanese rose, *R. multiflora.* Today it has to a considerable degree been superseded by its own descendant, the floribunda. Yet polyanthas have many sterling qualities and are still widely grown, especially for massing in beds, for they are very hardy low-growing plants and bear large clusters of small flowers throughout the summer and fall. Polyanthas are widely grown by florists as pot plants for Easter and Mother's Day sales. Such plants may be set into the garden with every expectation that they will live and grow for many years. One I set out by a mailbox is still thriving after 18 years despite the dust of summer and the onslaught of snow-melting chemicals in the winter.

Like the polyanthas, the hybrid perpetual roses have lost out in favor of their offspring—in this case the hybrid teas. But the hybrid perpetuals, which also have tea roses among their ancestors, are tall, handsome, big-flowered plants, usually hardier than the hybrid teas. Their development in the early part of the 19th Century marked the end of an era. Those roses that preceded them are known as old roses, while hybrid perpetuals and others developed

HOW TO TIE UP A CLIMBER

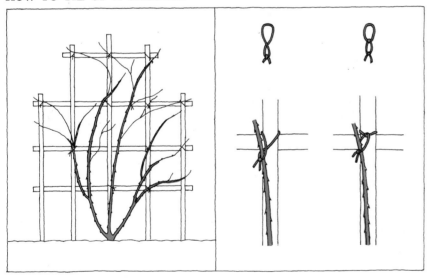

Because climbing roses lack the tendrils or "holdfasts" of true vines, they must be tied to a support such as a trellis, preferably in a fan shape. This arrangement stimulates more and better-distributed blossoms.

To tie a climber, loop string in a figure eight around the support and cane or stem before knotting (left). A more secure way is to tie the string around the support first, then again, loosely, around the stem (right).

since are called modern roses. They were tremendously popular for more than 50 years—in the 1880s one nurseryman alone listed over 800 varieties—for they combined huge and often intensely fragrant blossoms with hardiness, and many varieties bloomed repeatedly to provide flowers beyond the normal season. The name hybrid perpetual promises somewhat more than it delivers, however. Fully 90 per cent of the blossoms arrive at the first flush of bloom in early summer, and at that time hybrid perpetuals are the most colorful plants in the garden. Some varieties put forth a second, lighter display with the arrival of fall, and a few offer occasional flowers during the intervening period. Many gardeners today still prefer this schedule of flowering rather than the more regular production of hybrid teas.

The tea rose, *Rosa odorata,* originated countless years ago, probably from *R. chinensis,* the China, Bengal or monthly rose. Its climbing form derived from *R. odorata gigantea,* a climber from Burma and southwestern China that may grow 40 feet tall and bear blossoms 5 inches across. The varieties first brought to Europe from the Far East were double-flowering hybrids from gardens in the Orient, and they were given their name because many of them had a fragrance reminiscent of a newly emptied tea chest. Their colors range from white and blush to clear pink and various shades of yellow, including lemon, sulfur, apricot, buff, fawn and salmon. Tea roses bloom almost continuously and are slow to become dormant with the approach of cold weather. Thus they are easily killed by a sudden frost and are best suited to warm climates (Zones 8-10). Unlike hybrid teas, true tea roses grow well on their own roots and are often propagated from cuttings rather than from budding on other rootstalks.

For convenience, many other veterans of historic rose gardens are grouped in the general category of old roses, though in many cases they are unrelated or obscurely related, and some of them are newly bred additions to their types. Among the old roses are such plants as the pale alba rose; the moss rose, which secretes a substance that makes the buds sticky to touch but redolent of balsam; the cabbage or Provence rose, fragrant and many-petaled; the musk rose; the very ancient damask rose and the Noisette rose. Many of these have exotic flowers and a powerful fragrance, and their graceful, arching canes make an interesting contrast to the stiff, upright modern hybrids.

The ninth major grouping may be designated special-purpose roses. One such plant, the so-called tree rose, consists of almost any variety of rose plant grafted onto a tall main stem, or standard which usually requires a strong stake for support. The height of the lower plant determines how tall a tree rose will be; most are 2 to 5

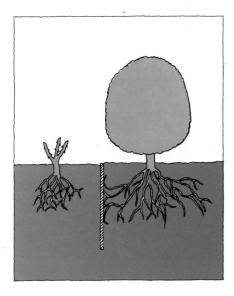

PROTECTING A ROSE'S ROOTS

Because roses are more vulnerable than most garden plants to competition from the invading roots of their neighbors, they need special protection when the plants are grown in front of shrubs or hedges such as privet, boxwood or yew—as they often are to show off their blossoms against a solid background of green. Before planting roses in a bed bordered by shrubs, excavate the bed and line the side toward the roses with a vertical shield of anodized aluminum or galvanized metal sheeting 18 to 24 inches wide, which can be purchased at some garden supply centers and at building supply or hardware stores.

feet tall, and, grown singly or in small groups in a prominent location, their effect is sensational. At the other end of the size scale is the miniature, or fairy, rose. The miniatures, many of them less than 1 foot high, are very hardy, continuously blooming rosebushes with perfect flowers about the size of a man's thumbnail. They serve very well in window boxes, rock gardens or in pots indoors.

Also included in this group are the shrub roses. For the most part they are species of wild roses, extremely hardy, vigorous and easy to maintain. A row of small shrub roses 3 or 4 feet tall makes an excellent garden boundary marker. While most shrub roses are handsome additions to any garden, a few species are too large for garden use. The multiflora, or Japanese, rose sends out such tall, dense, thorny growth that a hedgerow of the plants may reach 10 feet in height and 15 in thickness—but it will keep out any intruder larger than a rabbit.

Varied though the kinds of roses are, they are all members of one genus, with requirements for cultivation that set them apart from other plants. It is only natural for new gardeners to think that, because roses grow on bushes, they can grow under conditions that are suitable for other shrubs. But only some shrub roses are tough enough to grow with a minimum of soil preparation. Rosebushes' need for a certain amount of coddling comes from their unique hybrid background, since tender warm-climate plants are among their ancestors. Modern roses simply do not have the ability to grow as wild plants.

Another reason that roses need special attention is that they are extremely susceptible to root competition from other plants.

THE NEEDS OF ROSES

Tree roots are especially troublesome to roses, and when they are grown near trees, the tree roots must be sealed off from the rose bed with metal shields. Roses cannot compete well with many perennials, although some gardeners endeavor to combine the two types of plants in a border. To grow outstanding roses, plant them in a well-prepared bed by themselves.

The best place to grow roses is in full sunshine, for plants grown in the sun produce more flowers faster, and the bushes are apt to be sturdier. But almost any garden site that receives at least five to six hours of sunshine daily is suited for rose growing. Roses do not need sunshine all day long; a partially shaded area helps protect flower colors from fading. Early morning sun is to be preferred to afternoon sun, since it affords the plants an opportunity to dry off early in the day, thus cutting down on the incidence of leaf diseases common under moist conditions.

Good drainage is absolutely essential. Underground moisture, whether it comes from rain or conscientious watering, must not be allowed to accumulate at root level, for rose plants with "wet feet" can literally drown; roots need air as well as moisture. If a garden site that is otherwise acceptable lacks enough elevation to drain off naturally, its drainage can be improved by artificial means when the bed is prepared *(below)*. But the drainage of cold air is almost as important. Since cold air is heavier than warm air and will seek the lowest level, rose gardens should not be located in hollows. Many plants have died in frost pockets filled with stagnant cold air, while bushes only a few yards above them have come through without injury.

A garden site that is in the path of clearing breezes will be freed of dangerous frost pockets, but its plants may be heavily damaged by the breezes themselves, especially in winter. A moderate wind can quickly dry out exposed rose stems and whip long canes about, loosening the plants' roots. For these reasons, a good garden site will be open yet not fully exposed. Adequate windbreaks may be provided by a fence, a hedgerow or sturdy evergreens.

Finally, the gardener must make sure that his chosen garden site has the kind of soil that roses need to do their best. It has been said that any soil able to grow good corn will also grow good roses, but this is not a very helpful definition for suburbanites who have never grown corn.

The truth of the matter is that roses can be grown in almost any soil, but the soil may have to be modified. In some places—such as a few alkaline areas of the the West—the modification becomes extreme, requiring total replacement of existing soil to a depth of two feet. Almost everywhere, some minor adjustment of soil acidity is desirable, as is the addition of organic materials to improve soil texture, and fertilizer to add nutrients. Just how much modification your soil needs can be determined by testing it with a kit available at garden supply stores, or, for a more complete analysis, by sending a sample to the nearest office of your county agricultural extension service or a commercial soil-testing laboratory. Make no soil modification unless the test proves it necessary.

Roses do best in rather "heavy" soils—those that are mostly clay—to which an abundance of organic matter has been added to loosen the texture and help moisture drain away. If the soil is "light" —very sandy—even more organic matter should be added, for it prevents moisture from draining away too fast as well as too slowly. Of all the sources of organic matter, none suits roses more than well-rotted cow manure, but dried manure, ground peat moss or a compost made from decayed leaves will do. To help the plants grow strong roots, phosphorus compounds should also be mixed into the soil. Some gardeners use 20 per cent superphosphate, applied at the rate of 3 or 4 pounds per 100 square feet of garden area. Steamed bone meal is an alternative source of phosphorus, and may be applied at a rate of 3 to 6 pounds per 100 square feet. However, I prefer to use superphosphate since it gives you much more nourishment for your money.

Roses, like most garden plants, do best in soil that is very slightly acid—in terms of the numerical pH scale that is marked on the gauges of soil-testing kits, between 6.0 and 6.8 (7.0 is neutral and lower numbers indicate acidity, higher numbers alkalinity). For soils of average consistency, the pH can be raised 1 point —say, from 5.5 to 6.5—by adding 5 pounds of ground limestone per 100 square feet of garden area. To lower the pH ½ to 1 point, add 3 pounds of iron sulfate or ½ pound ground sulfur per 100 square feet.

None of these soil additives takes the place of the fertilizers that must be provided to nourish plants into vigorous bloom during the growing season (Chapter 2). The additives are needed to prepare the bed for planting and they require some time to act on the soil. Therefore it is best to construct the bed several months before the actual planting will be done. In the North (Zones 3-5), where roses are usually planted in the spring, the bed should be prepared in the late fall, just before the ground freezes. In the more moderate climates of Zones 6 and 7, roses may be planted either in the late fall or early spring; if they are to be set out in the fall it is advisable to prepare the garden in midsummer. Preparation in early fall is advisable in the warm climates of Zones 8-10, where roses are generally planted when they are most nearly dormant—that is, in December, January or February.

The first step is to mark the outline of the bed. Of course its

BUILT-IN WATERING FOR DRY LOCATIONS

In hot, dry areas where roses require almost daily watering, a buried system saves work, and water, by getting moisture directly to the roots. Dig the bed to a depth of 2 feet and lay 2 inches of coarse gravel. Connect sections of 3- or 4-inch-diameter perforated composition pipe the length of the bed. Cap one end and extend the other, by using an elbow and unperforated sections, to ground level; this end, fitted with a strainer, is supplied with water from a hose. Cover the pipe with 2 inches of gravel and refill the bed.

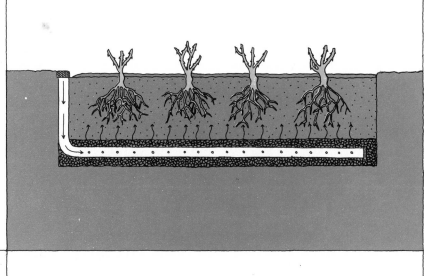

BUILT-IN DRAINAGE FOR WET LOCATIONS

In damp areas—for example, where heavy clay soil retains so much water that rose plants may drown—a drain pipe under the bed will carry off excess water, provided it can empty at a lower level. Dig a trench 2 feet deep along the length of the rose bed and extend it to the downhill exit. Lay 2 inches of gravel in the trench, place 3- or 4-inch-diameter perforated pipe in position, and cover with another 2 inches of gravel before replacing the soil.

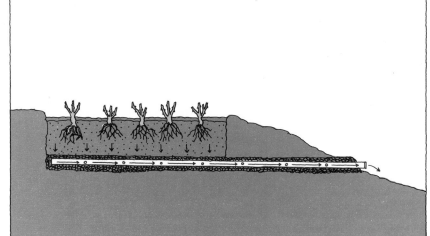

size and shape depend largely on the space available and personal taste but, unless the bed can be reached from two sides, it is wise to limit its width to no more than 5 feet. Then you can reach in among your plants to care for them properly, especially for spraying and dusting. If you want a wider bed, allow room for a footpath down the middle so you can reach all the plants easily.

Rose roots penetrate deeply into the soil, and for that reason it is necessary to prepare the soil much more deeply than one would for many other types of plants. I am of the opinion that one does not have to go to extremes in gardening and that it is not necessary to dig the soil to a depth of 4 feet, as was at one time advocated. Neither can you expect to have lovely roses if you simply scratch a hole in the ground and cram the roots into it. A well-prepared bed for roses should be excavated to a depth of 18 to 24 inches. Before digging, lay a tarpaulin, heavy paper or plastic on the grass beside the rose bed so that the soil can be piled on it. When the job is completed, the covering can be shaken free of soil, and the grass will still be clean. In digging the bed, first take off the sod and lay it to one side in a pile. Next, dig out the topsoil, which is darker in color than the subsoil beneath it, and pile it separately, and then remove as much subsoil as necessary.

At this point it is necessary to decide whether or not special drainage is required in order to keep water from standing in the bed during wet times of the year. If drainage must be provided from a sloping site, lay tile or composition drainage pipes in a trench from the bottom of the bed to a lower area. But there is no sense whatsoever in digging a bed in a wet area and putting in drains without having a lower area into which the water can flow; all you end up with is a sort of bathtub filled with water. When no such elevation differential exists, the only way to keep the soil well drained is to raise the rose bed above the general level of the soil around it. In parts of the Gulf Coast, for example, where there is a lot of rainfall and relatively level, poorly drained land, rose beds, as well as those of many other types of flowers, are normally elevated above the surrounding garden paths.

PROVIDING SPECIAL DRAINAGE

Now comes the time to enrich the bed with the preparations previously discussed. First of all, if the garden site was formerly under grass, take the sods and lay them upside down on the bottom of the bed. The idea here, and in the operations that follow, is to get the surface materials, which are richer in organic content, down to the plants' roots, which will need all the nourishment they can get. Then the pile of topsoil is mixed with the organic additives—one third by volume—and spread evenly on top of the sods, and tamped down firmly but not compressed. Finally, the pile of subsoil is mixed with more organic additives, and with superphosphate or bone meal. When the enriched subsoil is replaced and tamped down, your new rose garden will be full to overflowing. But the bed will have at least three months in which to settle and mellow before the time for planting arrives.

ENRICHING THE BED

This long waiting period gives you plenty of time for the rose grower's off-season sport—poring over lists and catalogues to select the varieties that will be planted. The pictures of blossoms are always entrancing, but some very practical considerations should be kept in mind: winter hardiness (particularly in Zones 3-5), disease resistance, ease of maintenance, and plant size. These factors have all been taken into account in the annotated listings of Chapter 4. The

HOW TO BUY ROSES

varieties described are plants that I have found to be particularly noteworthy. Two other guides to good varieties are also helpful. One is provided by All-America Rose Selections, Incorporated, an association of rose growers and nurserymen which test-grows new varieties and endorses a few of the best; the AARS endorsement is marked on rose packages. The other guide is the rating provided by the American Rose Society, which grades rose varieties on a numerical scale. A rating of 10.0 would be perfect, and one variety, the silvery pink moss rose Jeanne de Montfort, came close to that ideal, scoring 9.9. However, any variety rated 8.0 or higher is a good choice (annual ratings for all varieties can be obtained at small cost by writing to the society at P.O. Box 30,000, Shreveport, Louisiana 71130).

There is a wide variation in the quality of individual rosebushes of the same type, of course. To assure yourself of the best plants, deal with a reputable seller and look on the package labels for the quality-grade markings established by the American Association of Nurserymen. The best plants of each variety are rated Number 1, while lesser plants are graded Number 1½ or Number 2. The roots and canes of Number 1 roses will be bigger, better developed and more numerous than those of lower-rated plants. (Specific factors considered in rating four groups of roses are shown

STANDARDS FOR ROSEBUSHES

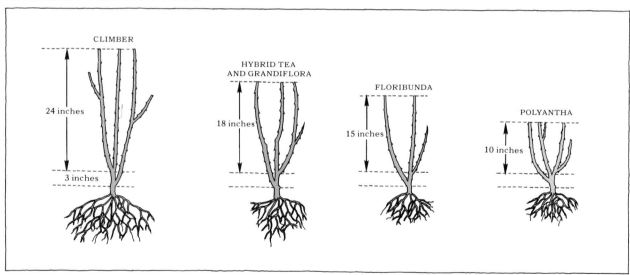

Rosebushes are graded 1, 1½ or 2, according to standards set for each of the types shown by the American Association of Nurserymen. To be rated No. 1, a hybrid tea, for example, must meet these requirements: when it is taken from the field it must be two years old and have three or more strong canes, two of which are 18 inches or longer, branching not higher than 3 inches above the knob of the bud union. The canes will not appear that long when the plant is bought because they will have been pruned to prevent breakage in handling and to keep the canes in balance with the root structure, some of which is cut off during the harvesting process.

in the illustration on page 20.) Since the price differential between a Number 1 and a Number 2 plant is not very great, I recommend that you ask for Number 1. The gardener who looks for bargains is likely to end up with a number of weak, undersized bushes. He may labor all summer to coax them along, but a Number 1½ or Number 2 bush will never equal a Number 1 in quantity or quality of flowers.

What the bushes look like when you actually buy them is determined by marketing practices. Rose plants are taken from the fields of the original growers when they are most nearly dormant and any remaining leaves can be removed (in some nurseries this chore used to be accomplished by letting a flock of sheep browse through the rose fields; now mechanical defoliators are used). At this point, the plant's bare roots are wrapped in moisture-preserving materials and the plants are put into protective packages for shipment to dealers and to mail-order buyers. The bare-root bushes must be planted before warm weather starts them growing again or they will die. Many dealers plant some bushes in pots to extend the selling season; potted bushes can be safely transplanted at any time, even while they are in full flower, and this makes them valuable as replacements for midseason casualties. But most rosebushes are sold in bare-root form and planted before the dormancy period ends in the spring.

Although planting time varies from place to place, you can buy your roses without undue worry about missing the local planting season. If you order in advance from a large mail-order house, even one in a distant state, your selection will be shipped to arrive at planting time in your area. If you prefer to wait until plants are available in local outlets and then buy in person, you will probably find a smaller selection, but in compensation the dealer has—and will share—valuable experience with rose-growing problems in your area.

Because most plants come concealed in their protective packages, you will probably see your roses for the first time when you unwrap them at home. You can tell at once if you bought high-quality plants. A good bush will have several plump, fresh, greenish canes; shriveled or discolored wood is usually a sign of dehydrated tissue. It will have several plump roots well distributed around the plant; the roots will be long and unbroken except perhaps for minor damage at one or two ends. Even the best bushes, however, will look rather strange to a beginning gardener. They are flowerless and leafless, with scraggly, sprawling roots, and it may seem highly unlikely that they will ever grow again. Yet from these unpromising bits of woody tissue will come blooms of unsurpassed beauty, and in only a few weeks.

ROSES THAT ARE NOT ROSES
Many plants having "rose" as part of their names are not related to the rose family at all, but are associated with it because of the shape or color of their blooms. The Christmas rose, for example, is an evergreen perennial whose white blossoms turn a roselike pink in winter. Rose mallow is another name for the stately hibiscus. Rose moss (not to be confused with the moss rose), is an annual of the portulaca genus with roselike flowers, and rose-of-heaven is a member of the pink family that boasts handsome, rose-colored flowers. Rose of Sharon, named after the Biblical plain, is actually a type of hibiscus with showy pink blossoms.

Royal families

Centuries of crossbreeding, accelerated by the development of scientific techniques in the 19th Century, have transformed the rosebushes of antiquity into a vast, interrelated lineage of flowers that today consists of many types, and numbers more than 13,000 identifiable varieties. The best-known and most popular of these are the hybrid tea roses, which account for virtually all of the cut roses sold by florists and for about three quarters of all roses produced commercially for gardens. Their popularity is understandable: they have long, pointed buds that open into large, symmetrical blossoms formed by the overlapping of many dozens of gracefully curving petals *(right)*. And in color they span the spectrum from white through every conceivable shade of pink, yellow and red to a maroon so deep as to appear almost black.

Between the sophisticated hybrid teas and their wild ancestors—some of which are still grown in gardens—are a host of other, less well-known roses. Among them is to be found virtually every characteristic that it is possible to breed into a flower. There are roses that stand erect, crawl along the ground, branch out to form magnificent hedges and cover entire walls. Some roses never grow more than a few inches high, while a few climbing varieties can reach 45 feet when tied to a fence or the side of a building for support. There are roses that produce dainty clusters of little flowers, each no bigger than a penny, and there are hybrid perpetuals that boast flowers as big as a man's face. Many roses have delightful fragrances reminiscent of tea, nuts, fruit, spices and honey, although there are a few that bring to mind the less pleasant aroma of stale beer or linseed oil. Others have completely lost their fragrances in the complicated breeding process that has also, surprisingly, produced some thornless roses.

Yet sweetly scented or odorless, large or small, prickly or smooth, delicately colored or dazzling in intensity, all roses share a common ancestral trait—a distinctive and memorable beauty that has earned for them the place of honor in the gardens of millions of flower lovers throughout the world.

In its unfolding petals, a hybrid tea rose displays the velvety texture, veining and rich color that make its type so popular.

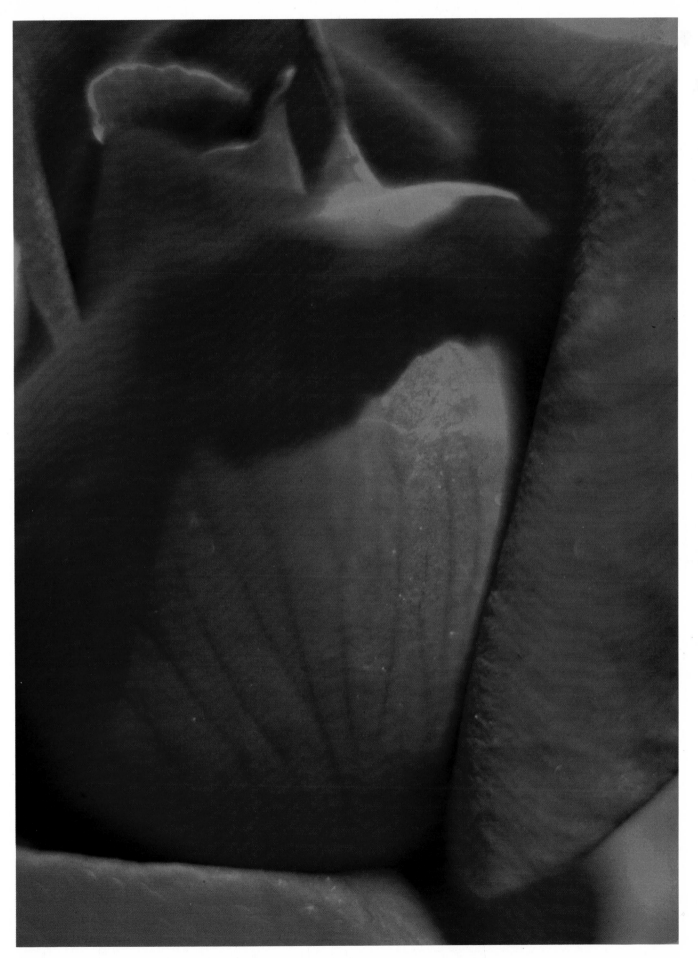

*A bee's-eye view of a Rosa spinosissima hybrid called **Frühlingsgold** (Spring Gold) reveals a mass of pollen-tipped stamens.*

The hardiest roses are the 200 or so wild or nearly wild varieties, called species roses, that are scattered around the world. Most of them are distinguished by their tall, shrublike growth and some are classified as shrub roses, others as climbers. They are usually easy to grow, and most bear five-petaled, intensely fragrant flowers that burst forth briefly each spring, occasionally repeating in the fall. While it is possible to transplant to home gardens some handsome varieties in their native state—*Rosa rugosa (below, left)* is an example—many wild roses are actually domesticated versions long cultivated in gardens, and some are man-made hybrids. By carefully matching types, breeders have been able to retain the charm of the wild rose while adding some wrinkles that nature never got around to, as in the golden version of *Rosa spinosissima (left)* and the long trailing variety known as Max Graf *(overleaf)*.

The reliable and hardy wild roses

A purplish red Rosa rugosa rubra (above) grows wild near a sandy Nantucket beach. An unusually rugged variety of species rose that thrives in cool weather in almost any kind of soil, Rosa rugosa is often found growing near the seashore since it is one of the few plants not injured by salt spray.

The orange-yellow Rosa foetida bicolor (above, right), also known as Austrian Copper, has been called the most beautiful wild rose. A chance mutation of an all-yellow rose, it was originally brought to Europe before the 13th Century by the Moors who invaded Spain from Africa.

Clusters of pink blossoms adorn the long, flexible canes of Max Graf (right), a species hybrid that was created by crossing the tall, erect Rosa rugosa with the shorter, ground-hugging Rosa wichuraiana. The result is a long trailing rose that is widely used in landscape gardening (overleaf).

A hedgelike mass of Max Graf trailing roses, a species hybrid, provides a formal garden with a bushy border that sparkles

with delicate color. In addition to the species roses, the garden includes red and white climbers secured to pillars and trellises.

The king-sized hybrid perpetuals

Floral relics usually associated with Victorian England, where they achieved their greatest popularity, the hybrid perpetual roses are spectacularly large and full; the blooms of one variety, Paul Neyron, measure up to 7 inches in diameter and another, Prince Camille de Rohan, has blossoms with as many as 100 petals. The hybrid perpetuals (so named because they bloomed more frequently than earlier types) were the first of the modern hybrid roses, the result of many crossings and recrossings of various roses, especially those of the damask and China types. Although 19th Century rose growers eventually developed more than 3,000 varieties, the hybrid perpetuals were virtually eclipsed by the newer, more colorful and more regularly blooming hybrid tea roses after the turn of the century. But even today their superior cold resistance makes them a good choice for gardens in cool climates.

Pink and scarlet streaks mark a Ferdinand Pichard rose, one of the few hybrid perpetuals developed in this century. This variety grows 5 to 6 feet high, but is often pruned shorter and then trained to form a low, spreading bush.

A dramatic hybrid perpetual is J. B. Clark (right). It bears large, handsome flowers, and its canes grow so long—8 to 10 feet—that in some gardens they must be tied to vertical supports, like the canes of a climbing rose.

The prolific floribundas

The hardy floribunda roses, with their large, distinctive clusters of flowers, are the result of the crossing by a Danish rose breeder of the beautiful but relatively fragile hybrid tea rose with the sturdy polyantha, a dwarf rose noted for its dense bunches of tiny blossoms. Since then the floribundas have become second only to the hybrid teas in popularity among rose gardeners. Today hundreds of varieties fill gardens with great puffs of color all summer long, and are often used as informal hedges and as borders for sidewalks, walls and building foundations.

The five-petaled flowers of Betty Prior (above), a popular floribunda rose, resemble the four-petaled blooms of pink dogwood, and have a pleasant, spicy fragrance. Like many older floribundas, this variety is usually grown as a shrub or as a hedge. It was introduced in 1938.

Europeana is one of the newer floribundas bred to provide handsome flowers suitable for cutting. A single cut stem can supply an instant bouquet of nearly two dozen large, brilliant red blossoms like those shown at right, each one containing as many as 25 to 30 ruffled petals.